# GREAT SCIENTIFIC THEORIES

# Evolution

## Nick Hunter

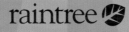
raintree

a Capstone company — publishers for children

Raintree is an imprint of Capstone Global Library Limited, a company incorporated in England and Wales having its registered office at 264 Banbury Road, Oxford, OX2 7DY – Registered company number: 6695582

**www.raintree.co.uk**
myorders@raintree.co.uk

Text © Capstone Global Library Limited 2018
First published in paperback in 2019
The moral rights of the proprietor have been asserted.

Edited by Helen Cox Cannons
Designed by Terri Poburka
Original illustrations © Capstone Global Library Limited 2017
Picture research by Morgan Walters
Production by Steve Walker
Originated by Capstone Global Library Limited
Printed and bound in India

ISBN 978 1 4747 4608 3 (hardback)
21  20  19  18  17
10 9 8 7 6 5 4 3 2 1

ISBN 978 1 4747 4613 7 (paperback)
22  21  20  19  18
10 9 8 7 6 5 4 3 2 1

**British Library Cataloguing in Publication Data**
A full catalogue record for this book is available from the British Library.

**Acknowledgements**
We would like to thank the following for permission to reproduce photographs: Alamy Images: Classic Image, 8, The Natural History Museum, 18; Getty Images Science & Society Picture Library, 24; Newscom: akg-images, 11, Album/Prisma, 20, Ann Ronan Picture Library Heritage Images, 17, Jewish Chronicle Heritage Images, 25, Pictures From History, 12, 16, The Print Collector Heritage Images, 21, World History Archive, 22; Science Source: Wellcome Images, 14; Shutterstock: Arevik, design element (textured paper), Chris Watson, 15, Dmitri Gomon, 26, Everett Historical, 28 (middle left), fixer00, design element (lines), Georgios Kollidas, 9, Giovanni Cancemi, cover, 23, Golden Shrimp, cover, design element (mathematical background), idiz, 19, Johan Swanepoel, 28 (top), Joseph Sohm, 27, Master3D, 28 (bottom), Rawpixel.com, 7, royaltystockphoto.com, 4, Sarunyu L, 5, Stephaniellen, 6, Wire_man, 10; Wikimedia: Sémhur / Wikimedia Commons/CC-BY-SA-3.0 (or Free Art License), 13.

We would like to thank Michael Bright for his invaluable help in the preparation of this book.

# CONTENTS

Some words are shown in bold, **like this**.
You can find out what they mean by
looking in the glossary.

# TESTING THEORIES

Science is all about trying to explain the world around us. Scientists try to discover how everything works, from the tiniest **bacteria** to much more complex living things, such as you and me. **Theories** are used to try to answer some of the biggest questions about the Universe and life itself, such as where human beings come from.

## New ideas

For hundreds of years, scientists have tried to explain the world by coming up with ideas about the way things work. These scientific ideas are known as hypotheses. When scientists believe they have collected enough **evidence** to show their idea is correct, the idea becomes a theory.

Living things include bacteria, which we can only see with a microscope.

*Evolution can help us to understand how extinct animals such as dinosaurs are related to animals that are still alive.*

## Theories

Scientists are testing new theories all the time, but their ideas are built on the theories of scientists who came before them. Some of history's greatest scientists changed the way people thought about the world.

## The theory of evolution

One of the biggest of these building blocks is the theory of **evolution**. The theory was developed separately by Charles Darwin and Alfred Russel Wallace during the 1800s. It explains how the millions of different types of animals and plants developed. But the story of the theory of evolution would not be complete without the contribution of many different scientists.

## THE FIRST SCIENTISTS

People have been studying science and developing theories since ancient times. However, the word "scientist" was not used until the 1830s.

# WHAT IS EVOLUTION?

Why are there so many different living things on Earth? Why do many animals seem to be designed to survive in extreme **environments**, such as deserts or the deep ocean? The **theory** of **evolution** answers these and many other questions.

## The beginning of life

Evolution explains how all forms of life on our planet developed from chemical substances that were present on Earth more than 3.5 billion years ago. Scientists cannot be sure what these substances were and when life first developed. However, they know that all living things developed from these first signs of life.

## SAME ANCESTOR

The first signs of human beings began around 2.8 million years ago. Humans and gorillas had the same **ancestor**.

All humans are part of the same species, but we do not all look exactly the same.

## Where do species come from?

A **species** is a group of animals with similar features that can produce **offspring**, or babies, together. Human beings are a single species. Each living thing is slightly different from its parents. These differences make some living things better able to survive. These survivors pass on their unique features to their own offspring. Over millions of years, these tiny changes lead to the development of new species. This is known as **natural selection** (see page 17).

## Learning more

Since the theory of evolution was explained, scientists have learned even more. They have been able to uncover the processes and chemicals inside living things that allow them to pass on features, such as hair colour, to their offspring.

# EARLY IDEAS ABOUT LIFE

Two hundred and fifty years ago, people in Europe believed that Earth was no more than 6,000 years old. This figure was not based on the age of rocks and other scientific **evidence**, but on religious beliefs and dates.

## THE START OF HISTORY?

Archbishop James Ussher (1581–1656) used the Bible and other Christian writings to work out that God created the world in the week before 23 October 4004 BC — just over 6,000 years ago. Scientists now agree that Earth is about 4.5 billion years old.

## A design for life

Christian churches taught that God created all **species** of animals and plants. They believed that humans were better than other animals, as they had a special place in God's creation. In 1802, British clergyman William Paley (1743–1805) wrote a book. In it, Paley claimed that the variety of the natural world could not have happened by chance, and must have been designed by God.

## Classifying life

During the 1600s and 1700s, scientists began to look at the natural world in more detail. Swedish scientist Carl Linnaeus (1707–1778) developed a system for classifying and naming living things according to their physical features. Linnaeus gave each species two names in Latin to show which groups they belonged to. For example, the full name of the domestic rabbit is *Oryctolagus cuniculus*. Linnaeus' system of **classification** is still in use today.

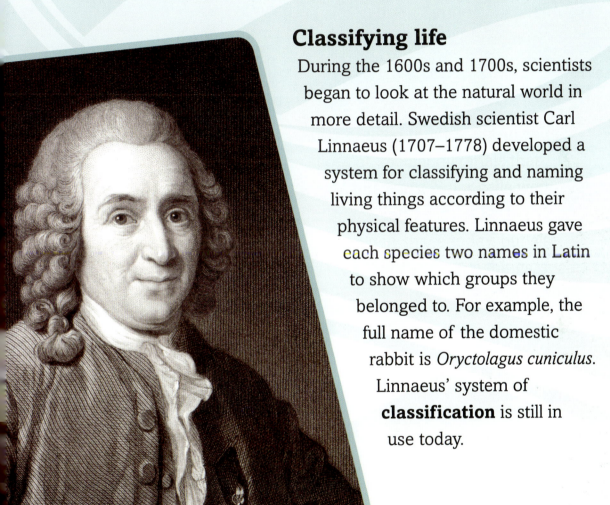

*Even as a young child, Carl Linnaeus was fascinated by the names of plants. He memorized as many names as he could.*

## First ideas about evolution

By the 1700s, some scientists started to question the common view of Earth's history. If Earth was only created a few thousand years ago, they wondered, how can we explain the **fossil** remains of animals that were clearly far older?

## Gradual change

**Geologists** study rocks and minerals that make up our planet. The ideas of Scottish geologist Charles Lyell (1797–1875) had a big effect on **naturalists**. Lyell worked out that Earth's surface and landforms, such as mountains, had formed gradually over millions of years.

### WHAT CAN FOSSILS TELL US?

Fossils are the remains of animals naturally preserved in stone over millions of years. Studying fossils can help us to understand animals that lived in the past.

*Cliffs, such as these, have layers of rock. The layers show that the cliffs have slowly formed over millions of years.*

## Lamarck and evolution

Scientists studying the natural world also started to work on **theories** about how living things change and new species are born. French scientist Jean-Baptiste Lamarck (1744–1829) developed the first theory of **evolution** around 1801. Lamarck was convinced that different species of living things **evolved**, or changed gradually, over time. But his idea that living things changed themselves to fit their **environment** was incorrect. In fact, changes in living things take place over many **generations**. How evolution happened was the missing piece of the puzzle.

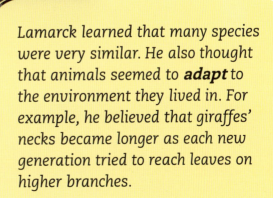

Lamarck learned that many species were very similar. He also thought that animals seemed to **adapt** to the environment they lived in. For example, he believed that giraffes' necks became longer as each new generation tried to reach leaves on higher branches.

# DARWIN AND NATURAL SELECTION

The young English **naturalist** Charles Darwin (1809–1882) was fascinated by nature and the world around him from a very young age. He loved the animals that lived next to the river near his home in Shrewsbury.

## Decisions

As a young man, Darwin could not decide what he wanted to do with his life. He studied medicine, but changed his mind. He went to Cambridge University, where he studied to be a priest. While at Cambridge, Darwin was much more interested in attending classes about science and nature.

*This portrait of Darwin was painted in 1840, at the time he was working on his theory to explain **evolution**.*

## The voyage of the *Beagle*

In 1831, aged just 21, Darwin was offered the chance to join the crew of HMS *Beagle*. Darwin would be a "scientific person" and guest of the ship's captain on a round-the-world voyage. As well as exploring distant parts of the world, Darwin would be able to study living things in many different **environments**. These included the tropical rainforests of South America and isolated islands in the Pacific Ocean. The voyage lasted five years. Darwin later wrote that it was "by far the most important event in my life".

## EARTH-SHAKING EVENTS

Darwin did not just study animals on his voyage. In Chile, South America, he saw a volcano erupt and was caught in an earthquake. This convinced him that ideas about how Earth's surface is constantly changing were correct.

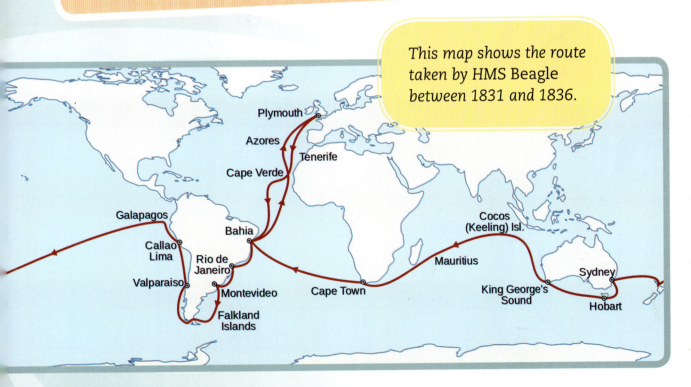

This map shows the route taken by HMS Beagle between 1831 and 1836.

## Investigating life

The voyage of HMS *Beagle* was not just an important event in Darwin's life. What Darwin learned changed people's understanding of the natural world.

## Exploration

As the ship explored the coast of South America, Darwin filled his notebooks with observations about every kind of plant and animal. He collected thousands of **specimens** too, which he sent back to England.

The **fossils** he found in South America fascinated Darwin. He could see that these extinct animals were similar to animals still living on the continent. He started to think that there could be a link between them.

22    STRUCTURE OF    CHAP. I.

Fig. III.

ORCHIS PYRAMIDALIS.

*We know so much about the voyage of HMS Beagle because of Darwin's own writings and sketches, such as this one.*

## Galápagos Islands

The Galápagos Islands are in the Pacific Ocean, around 1,000 kilometres from South America. They are home to many **species** of animals not found anywhere else. Darwin discovered that species of birds found on the islands were different to those he had seen in South America. The species also differed between different islands of the Galápagos.

*The Galápagos penguin is a species of penguin that is only found in the Galápagos.*

## Returning home

When Darwin returned home in 1836, he was well known among fellow **naturalists**. Others had studied the amazing specimens he had collected. In 1839, Darwin published the journals of his voyage. The journals did not include anything about evolution, but the book soon became a bestseller.

**Breakthrough moment**

## DANGEROUS IDEAS

It took several years of study before Darwin worked out the great **theory** of evolution. He first wrote a short paper explaining his ideas in 1842, but he was not yet ready to share it with the public. Darwin knew that his theory would cause a sensation.

## Theory of evolution by natural selection

More than 20 years passed before Darwin finally published his theory of evolution by **natural selection**. He had written the theory in the years following his life-changing voyage on HMS *Beagle*. But he arranged with his wife that the theory would only be published after his death. Darwin did not want to anger Christians with his theory.

## Life goes on

Darwin moved with his family to Down House in Kent. He wrote detailed studies of many areas of nature, including coral reefs and barnacles. He eventually decided to publish his theory in 1858 after receiving a letter from another naturalist – Alfred Russel Wallace (1823–1913).

## ALFRED RUSSEL WALLACE

Darwin and Wallace jointly published their theory of evolution by natural selection in 1858. Today, however, Darwin is much better known. During his lifetime, Wallace was very famous for his role in developing the theory.

16

## How natural selection works

Wallace had come up with the same theory of evolution as Darwin. Both naturalists believed that evolution happened because of natural selection. All living things have slightly different features, even if they are part of the same species. These features will be passed on to their **offspring**. However, not all living things will survive long enough to produce offspring.

## Adapting

Darwin concluded that only the animals that were best suited, or **adapted**, to their environment would survive to pass on their features. This meant that species of living things would change. Over many **generations**, this process would lead to new species.

These sketches of different species of finch were drawn by Darwin on his trip to the Galápagos. He noticed that they had different size beaks and heads.

1. Geospiza magnirostris.
2. Geospiza fortis.
3. Geospiza parvula.
4. Certhidea olivasca.

# A FURIOUS REACTION

In 1859, Charles Darwin's book *On the Origin of Species by Means of Natural Selection* was published. When Darwin and Wallace unveiled the **theory** to a scientific society in the previous year, hardly anyone noticed. But Darwin's book caused a huge reaction, and much of it was hostile.

## Attack

Darwin's theory questioned some of the most important ideas of his time. The book was attacked from many sides. Religious leaders did not like the fact that Darwin questioned their belief that all **species** had been created by God. Other scientists hated Darwin's ideas because he had proved all their theories were wrong.

## Defending Darwin

Darwin himself was ill, so he was unable to defend his theory. Other scientists stepped in. In 1860, at a public meeting in Oxford, Thomas Henry Huxley (1825–1895) defended Darwin's theory against attacks by the Bishop of Oxford.

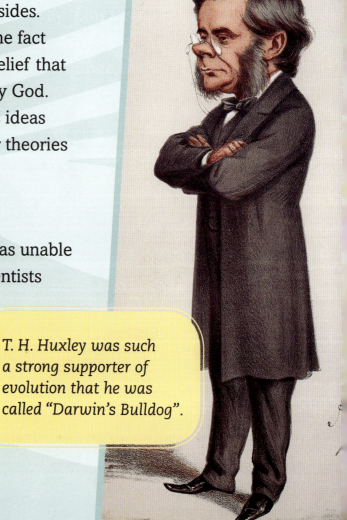

T. H. Huxley was such a strong supporter of evolution that he was called "Darwin's Bulldog".

Wallace tried to explain why many animals are only found in particular places. Kangaroos are only found in Australia because their ancestors were not able to move between distant continents.

## Evolution and geography

Scientists continued to argue over Darwin and Wallace's theory. But other scientists built on Darwin's ideas. Wallace went on to explore why different species existed in different places. He focused on how species differed between South Asia and Australia.

## Some agreement

By the end of the 19th century, most scientists agreed that **evolution** did take place. They also agreed that different species developed from common **ancestors**. However, even some of Darwin's supporters were not sure that **natural selection** was the cause of this process.

## Explaining human evolution

Much of the debate about Darwin's theories centred on whether human beings **evolved** in the same way as animals. Darwin deliberately avoided writing about this in his book. He worried that he would face an even angrier reaction if he dealt with human evolution.

## First human fossils

The first human **fossils** were only discovered in 1857. Before then, there was no **evidence** to prove that modern humans had evolved from other species. A skull was found by German miners in the Neander Valley. The early human ancestor the skull belonged to was later named Neanderthal Man. Fossils showed that Neanderthals were similar to modern humans but died out around 30,000 years ago.

*This cartoon shows Darwin as an ape. It makes fun of his ideas about human evolution.*

### The Descent of Man

In 1871, Darwin published *The Descent of Man*, setting out his ideas on human evolution. He wrote that all humans shared a common ancestor with apes, and that the first humans probably came from Africa. Once again, Darwin's ideas caused controversy. Even Alfred Russel Wallace believed that humans had not evolved in the same way as other animals.

## EUGENE DUBOIS

The question of human evolution could not be finally solved without fossils of early humans. **Geologist** Eugene Dubois (1858–1940) explored caves on the island of Java, now part of Indonesia. In 1890, he found the fossilized remains of a human-like creature that lived millions of years ago. Other scientists disagreed when Dubois claimed he had discovered a new human ancestor. Later discoveries proved he was right.

*Fossil discoveries have enabled scientists to understand the stages of human evolution.*

# GENETICS AND HEREDITY

Darwin's great **theory** explained how new **species** developed and that all living things shared **ancestors**. It was up to other scientists to explain how **characteristics** were passed from one **generation** to the next.

## Mendel's peas

Between 1856 and 1863, Austrian monk and scientist Gregor Mendel (1822–1884) carried out a series of experiments. These would be the basis of a new branch of science – **genetics**. His experiments involved pea plants. He worked out how the plants **reproduced** and passed on different characteristics to the new plants that grew from their seeds, such as the height of the plants. Mendel published his results in 1866. Few people understood them and they were mostly ignored.

Gregor Mendel's work was only rediscovered in the early 1900s, after his death.

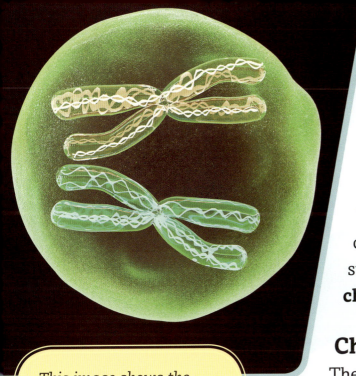

## Genetics and evolution

In the late 1800s, scientists started looking in detail at the tiny cells that make up all animals and plants. They discovered that each cell contained rod-shaped structures, which were named **chromosomes**.

*This image shows the structure of chromosomes. This can only be seen with a powerful microscope.*

## Chromosomes

The chromosomes in each living cell are made up of bundles of a substance called **DNA** (Deoxyribonucleic acid). These chromosomes contain the information that determines the features of individual animals and plants, such as eye colour. Chromosomes are passed from one generation to the next, which explains why **offspring** look like their parents.

## Breakthrough moment

## FRUIT FLIES

By studying millions of fruit flies, US scientist Thomas Hunt Morgan was able to see that **genes** could change, or **mutate**, suddenly. A mutated gene could then be passed on to future generations. Discoveries like this helped scientists to understand that Darwin was probably right.

## The importance of chromosomes

Scientists such as Thomas Hunt Morgan started to understand how important chromosomes and genes were in all living things. They contained information about each cell's features and passed on information from one generation to the next. However, scientists were still a long way from understanding the process itself.

## Structure of DNA

DNA was first discovered in the 1860s by Johann Friedrich Miescher. In 1944, American Oswald Avery discovered that the chemical substance that passed on information from one generation to the next in living things was DNA. The race then began to find out how this happened.

*James Watson and Francis Crick showed that the structure of DNA was a double helix, like a twisted ladder.*

## Breakthrough

In 1953, Francis Crick and James Watson revealed that they had pieced together the structure of DNA. This was a huge breakthrough in the field of genetics. Their discovery would not have been possible without the work of scientists Maurice Wilkins and Rosalind Franklin.

## Genetic sequencing

This great breakthrough has had a huge impact on modern science. Each living thing has slightly different genes. Today's scientists can explore the individual parts that make up these genes. They can now change individual genes to protect us from certain diseases, and change features of animals and plants.

## ROSALIND FRANKLIN

Rosalind Franklin (1920–1958) did her own experiments to unravel the structure of DNA, using X-rays. Watson and Crick used Rosalind Franklin's **pioneering** work in their studies of DNA, probably without her knowledge. Franklin was not given full credit for her part in this amazing discovery until after her death.

# WHY DOES EVOLUTION MATTER?

Two hundred years ago, few scientists understood where the huge variety of life on Earth came from. Today, scientists understand the process of **evolution**. Advances in technology also mean that we can influence evolution itself.

## Understanding life

It is important that we understand where we come from and how life has developed. However, understanding this also brings many benefits to our everyday lives.

## Environmental benefits

Humans are having a major impact on our planet, through pollution and climate change. Many **species** are dying out, but our knowledge of evolution may help us to find solutions. Coral reefs are very sensitive to rising ocean temperatures. But scientists may be able to develop types of coral that are less affected by these changes.

A mystery disease has hit honey bee numbers. Knowledge of genes could help us to protect this important species.

Diseases such as HIV/AIDS affect millions of people around the world. Scientists' work on DNA may offer some hope of a cure one day.

## Medical benefits

Scientists' understanding of **DNA** can help us to cure some diseases. By **genetically** modifying – or changing – plants, some plants are now being used to help fight disease. Modifications can also increase crops to provide food for some of our planet's poorest people.

## Future discoveries

If the history of science teaches us anything, it is that our current knowledge has limits. There are more discoveries to be made.

## CONCERNS

Our understanding of evolution and genetics can bring benefits, but many people are concerned. Our knowledge of **genes** can be used to tackle diseases and disabilities in humans. But would it be right if we used this to change human babies' hair colour or make them more clever?

# QUIZ

1. Archbishop James Ussher concluded that the world was created in which year?

2. Which types of animals did Jean-Baptiste Lamarck believe grew longer necks as each new **generation** was born?

3. What did Charles Darwin write was "by far the most important event" in his life?

4. Which islands in the Pacific Ocean had a big effect on Darwin's ideas?

5. Which **naturalist** wrote to Darwin explaining his own theory of **evolution** by **natural selection**?

6. Who was called "Darwin's Bulldog"?

7. Where were the first human **fossils** discovered?

8. On what plants did Gregor Mendel carry out thousands of experiments to find out how features were passed from one generation to the next?

9. Which discovery did James Watson and Francis Crick reveal in 1953?

10. Which woman played an important part in the discovery of the structure of **DNA**?

**For the answers to this quiz, see page 31**

# TIMELINE

**1707**   Birth of Carl Linnaeus, who **pioneered** the **classification** of living things

**1801**   Jean-Baptiste Lamarck sets out the first **theory** of evolution, although he did not know how **species** changed over time

**1802**   William Paley publishes the book *Natural Theology*, explaining how the natural world supported Christian beliefs

**1831**   Young naturalist Charles Darwin joins the crew of HMS *Beagle* for its voyage around the world via the coast of South America

**1836**   Darwin returns to Britain and begins to study the thousands of **specimens** he had sent home from the voyage

**1856**   Austrian monk and scientist Gregor Mendel begins experiments that would be the first steps in the science of **genetics**

**1857**   First human fossils discovered in Neander Valley, Germany

**1858**   Charles Darwin and Alfred Russel Wallace explain the theory of evolution by natural selection in papers presented to a group of scientists

**1859**   Darwin's book *On the Origin of Species by Natural Selection* is published. It becomes a bestseller but also causes an uproar.

**1944**   Oswald Avery discovers that DNA is the substance that passes on information from one generation to the next in living things

**1953**   James Watson and Francis Crick reveal the structure of DNA for the first time, with the help of research from Maurice Wilkins and Rosalind Franklin

# GLOSSARY

**adapt** change to fit a situation or environment

**ancestor** someone or something from a previous generation, for example, a great-grandparent

**bacteria** group of single-celled living things that can only be seen with a microscope

**characteristics** features that makes a person or thing different from others

**chromosome** bundles of molecules, including DNA, found in each living cell and used to pass on genetic information

**classification** arranging animals and plants into groups by similarities

**DNA** (Deoxyribonucleic acid) substance present in all living things that carries genetic information

**environment** surroundings in which a person, animal or plant lives

**evidence** collection of information or facts that prove if something is true or not

**evolution** way in which species of living things develop from earlier forms

**evolve** change gradually

**fossil** remains of an ancient animal or plant, found in rock

**gene** information that is passed from a parent to its offspring when the parent reproduces

**generation** group of people or animals born and living during the same time period

**genetics** study of genes and inherited characteristics in things

**geologist** person who studies the rocks and minerals on and beneath Earth's surface

**mutate** change, often used to describe unusual changes in genes

**natural selection** process in which living things that are best adapted to their environment survive and pass on their features to their offspring

**naturalist** person who observes and studies the natural world

**offspring** young of an animal or plant, such as human children

**pioneer** first person to apply or use a new method for doing something

**reproduce** produce offspring

**species** group of living things that are related to each other and can breed

**specimen** example or sample of something, collected in order to be studied by scientists

**theory** scientific idea with evidence to back it up

# FIND OUT MORE

## BOOKS

*Charles Darwin* (Scientists Who Made History), Cath Senker
(Wayland, 2014)

*Genetic Engineering: Should Humans Control Nature?* (Ask the Experts),
Leon Gray (Franklin Watts, 2015)

*The Story of Life: A First Book about Evolution*, Catherine Barr and Steve
Williams (Frances Lincoln Children's Books, 2015)

*What is Evolution?*, Louise Spilsbury (Wayland, 2016)

## WEBSITES

**www.bbc.co.uk/education/topics/z3pp34j/resources/1**
This BBC Bitesize website has lots of fascinating video clips about
evolution and inheritance. The videos cover topics such as why a giraffe
has a long neck, which animal is the best predator and why the brown
bear evolved into the polar bear.

**www.dkfindout.com/uk/history/stone-age/human-ancestors**
DK's Findout website includes information on human evolution.

**www.ngkids.co.uk/science-and-nature/charles-darwin-and-the-mystery-of-life**
Learn more about Darwin on National Geographic's website.

## ANSWERS TO QUIZ

**1.** 4004 BC; **2.** Giraffes; **3.** The voyage of HMS *Beagle*; **4.** The Galápagos Islands; **5.** Alfred Russel Wallace; **6.** Thomas Henry Huxley, because he defended Darwin's theory in public meetings; **7.** Neander Valley, Germany; **8.** Pea plants; **9.** The structure of DNA; **10.** Rosalind Franklin

# INDEX